Pages missing 10/2/17

VERANDA

The Romance of
Flowers

CHA

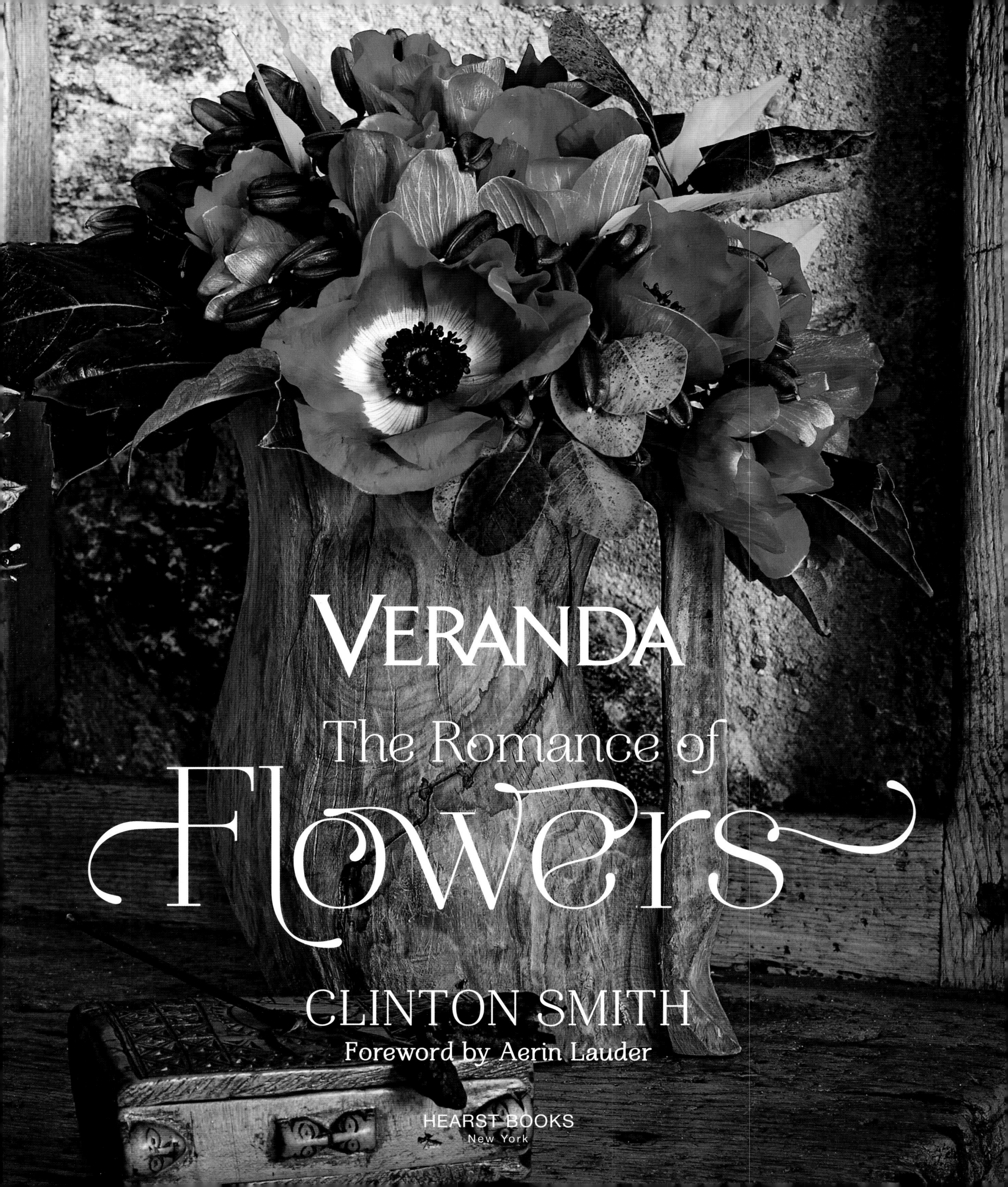

Veranda

The Romance of
Flowers

CLINTON SMITH

Foreword by Aerin Lauder

HEARST BOOKS
New York

This book is dedicated to the floral designers and interior designers who inspire us, and the homeowners, clients and patrons who champion their creativity.

Left: *White tulips, anemones, peonies and hydrangeas are as timeless as blue-and-white porcelain.*

Foreword

Flowers are part of my DNA. My grandmother, Estée Lauder, taught me many things . . . the love of family, a passion for work, and an appreciation for beauty in all its forms, from fashion to interior design to flowers. Her homes were always filled with beautiful arrangements, starting with white tuberoses or Casa Blanca lilies in the entry to welcome you with their incredible scent. ¶ As a little girl, I followed her example and put flowers on my desk. When my mother let me redo my bedroom, I picked floral fabrics rather than stripes. On my wedding day, I wore gardenias in my hair and carried a lily of the valley bouquet. I love white flowers, just as my grandmother did. She had a white cutting garden in East Hampton and now that I'm living in her house with my family, I've added

Right: *White flowers are always in style.*

to it, planting dahlias, peonies and roses. ¶ Clinton Smith, who worked diligently to write this book in between editing each issue of *Veranda*, tells wonderful stories about working beside his grandmother in her garden. I share similar fond memories that are recalled as I savor each page of this beautiful book. ¶ Flowers are also at the core of my own brand, AERIN. I've designed flower-shaped bowls, flower-bedecked sconces, and flower-strewn fabrics. Whenever I travel, I'm always taking pictures of the flowers in hotels and restaurants. In Hong Kong, I was dazzled by the flower market. In Vienna, I spotted edelweiss in the window of a florist and had to go in. Tokyo is the ultimate for cherry blossoms. Houses in the Bahamas are almost smothered in hibiscus. It looks so exuberant. Flowers can tell you a lot about a place.

I vividly remember picking wild blackberries along fencerows, and the annual spring visits to the local nurseries where we would discover geraniums in half a dozen colors, fruit trees, Boston ferns as big as a bed and azaleas as far as the eye could see. My MeeMaw's garden was where we planted zinnias from seed and, by season's end, they were taller than both of us—even when I was a teenager. My Big Mama's garden was where we planted pink impatiens and white petunias, and my parents' own yard was a veritable arboretum. Filled with six giant oak trees (some fifteen feet in circumference), two Japanese maples with fire-engine red leaves, a pecan tree, a fig tree, and a grand chestnut tree that has since been removed, this haven burst forth each spring with the bountiful blossoms of pink and white dogwoods, rose of Sharon and an intoxicat-

*Left: The romance of dahlias comes from their seemingly limitless colors and types. Rustic in the garden, they are easily elevated to elegant arrangements. **Overleaf:** An allée of blue hydrangeas.*

ing saucer magnolia. Even one of the first bylines I received as a journalist was related to flowers: it was a story about the creation of a Shakespearean garden, which included only plants and flowers featured in the playwright's works. ¶ While these memories center on flowers in their natural state, it is worth noting that while this isn't a gardening book, it's impossible to produce a book on flowers without considering their origin and purpose. Flowers represent the life force of plants; they are, in fact, their reproductive organs. Every bud, blossom and bloom featured within these pages is the glorious (and hardworking) appendage to what might otherwise be an unremarkable plant. Though the first life cycle of these beautiful objects may be concluded with a brisk snip or quick cut, they take on a vibrant second life with two simple ingredients: fresh

Right: *Pale pink peonies echo a trio of antique paintings.*
Overleaf, left: *A vibrant vase of yellow ranunculus.* **Overleaf, right:** *A red dahlia rises to the sun.*

water and a vessel to hold them. With a little imagination and some TLC, cut flowers bring weeks of additional joy. ¶ The romance of flowers is as emotional and complicated as any Shakespearean love sonnet. Take the peonies that grace a number of pages in this book, for instance. Is there anything more romantic? Perhaps a rose, but even that's debatable. Big, bold peony blossoms can stop traffic with their singular beauty, captivating scent, and abundant scale (often the size of a small dinner plate). It isn't uncommon for a peony tree to live for fifty years, although some can live upward of one hundred years. Yet as prolific and pleasing as this plant might be, it can be cantankerous. If the peony is uprooted and replanted, it might not bloom again for several years. What makes the flowers in this book so special is that they literally reflect the

Left: Crimson-colored peonies echo the room's rich, romantic color scheme.

art of living, and the expertise, adventure, craft and care (and patience) that goes into creating stunning floral arrangements truly constitutes an art form. ¶ That artistry has been at the heart of *Veranda's* makeup since the magazine's inception in 1987. Founder Lisa Newsom elevated floral design to new heights by showcasing beautiful arrangements in the same way she did the most stylish houses—with lush photography and expansive, gallery-like presentations. Newsom advocated the importance of flowers in our lives, as well as preserving our environment for future generations. As a result, the magazine has long championed the interplay between indoors and out—with outdoor rooms as elegant as any interior space, and interior rooms that harken to the great outdoors. Cut flowers have often served as the bridge that connects the two. ¶

Right: *An exotic odontoglossum orchid is juxtaposed with an 18th-century French chair in stately dishabille.*

While a magazine's ink-on-paper format doesn't allow readers to capture the true aroma of a flower in a photograph, the thoughts and remembrances that come from smelling a bouquet or a single stem is often as intimate of an experience as curling up with a favorite book or periodical. The waft of sweet jasmine can evoke a languorous weekend in New Orleans, just as a waft of eucalyptus can evoke long hikes through the redwood forests of Northern California. But sometimes there can be too much of a good thing: the scent from a cluster of tiger lilies on a dining table, for example, can overpower the aroma and taste of a fine meal, while the same flower would work splendidly elsewhere. A bouquet of them in a foyer provides a robust welcome to guests, and even a single stem on a bedside table offers up a sunny dose of morning cheer. ¶ Few things in this world hold as much symbolism as flowers. They commemorate every occasion in the cycle of our lives, beginning to end, in sickness and in health. Flowers mark the first flirtations of a new romance and adorn the bride and groom at their wedding. Flowers herald the birth of a new child and mark the passing of someone beloved. Flowers mark the rites of passage into adulthood, from *quinceaneras* to bat mitzvahs. Flowers can be solemn or celebratory. They can represent millions of unspoken thoughts, and inspire countless moments of reflection. ¶ Perhaps because they are living things that, in one sense, give their lives so that we may enjoy our own more, flowers seem to evoke powerful emotions and we seem to empathize with them on a humanistic level. Consider a pink dahlia bud as an infant, not yet unfurled and revealed to the world, not quite

Right: *Orange-red tulips add a fiery jolt of color and change the mood in a peaceful dining room.*
Overleaf: *Life imitates art with a bevy of brick-red peonies that echo the energy found in a bold contemporary photograph.*

ready to leave its mother. Or the eyes-wide-open enthusiasm of an adolescent red tulip, unfurling and revealing itself as it reaches towards the light. And then the quiet repose of a wilting white rose, as it slowly passes, dropping its petals delicately one at a time. These blossoms are a metaphor of our own life journeys and stand as markers for the feelings and emotional states we all inhabit. ¶ Today there is so much talk about how the Internet has made the world a smaller place, but let's not forget that the flower community was a pioneer in global communication: from the earliest trade routes at sea to the arrival of jet travel, the exchange of almost any sort of cut flower, decorative stem or ornamental foliage available could be realized most anywhere in the world. With the advent of flower-of-the-month clubs and wire services, tulips

Right: *A sophisticated arrangement of roses, hyacinths and lilies of the valley is perfectly balanced by a neoclassical vase.*

from the Netherlands, chrysanthemums from Columbia, and exotic protea from Australia have become as commonplace as bluebonnets in Texas or magnolias in Mississippi. Even the everyday grocery store and corner market have exotic specimens from around the globe. China and India are the two largest growers of flowers in the world, and have growing strategies that surpass the imagination. Yet as much as the world's flower markets offer the unusual and the unexpected, people are also now turning to their own backyards to weave together arrangements based simply on what's in season. The demand for flowers has never been greater, and the options for great floral designs remain unlimited. ¶ The creativity expressed in this book channels that ambition, with inventiveness, ingenuity, savvy and, of course, great style.

Right: *A vase wrapped in bark is an unexpected container for a pretty arrangement of jasmine, ranunculus, Japanese ranunculus and scabiosa.*

Fig. 12

Fig. 2

Fig. 3

Fig. 7

Fig. 1

Fig. 5

Fig. 6

Fig. 1 e

Glamorous
Stylish
Sophisticated

"Where are the cameras? Where are my flowers? I must be photographed with flowers! Get them before I'm surrounded by cameramen!"
—Mae Murray, silent-film star

Right: *Peonies, dahlias and sweet pea bring a touch of informality to a Chinese export vase. The porcelain pea pods add a whimsical touch.*

What makes certain flowers particularly stylish, sophisticated, even glamorous? Why does one stem sometimes so clearly distinguish itself from another, make itself somehow more alluring, more attractive than the rest? Whatever it may be, these sophisticated blooms possess the same indescribable qualities—you know-it-when-you-see-it—that distinguishes memorable legends of the silver screen. Think Marilyn Monroe, Lauren Bacall and Lana Turner. Their beauty is magnetic, awe-inspiring and one of a kind. Like them, these flowers often possess

Right: *A profusion of sweet peas en masse creates a dynamic focal point.* **Overleaf:** *White orchids are the only adornment required in a dining room that's enveloped in whimsical wallpaper featuring a floral motif.*

the sensuous curves, elusive mystique, or ineffable panache that makes it impossible to resist their allure. ¶ In the realm of flowers, as in film, certain blossoms may play in a supporting role, while others command center stage, acting as the heroine, diva, or femme fatale in a dramatic role. In a particularly powerful arrangement, it may be the strong, stalwart presence of a hollyhock, with its overscale blossoms and long stems, so simple, even sweet, yet tough as nails—commanding the performance as Gloria Swanson did when she portrayed Norma Desmond in *Sunset Boulevard*. In a more subtle yet equally powerful setting, it may be the fleeting blossom of a single magnolia, floating in a still bowl of water. With its singular beauty and fragrance as identifiable as a favorite perfume, its effect is powerful and as alluring as its costar. ¶ In the movie

Right: *Long stems of blush-colored tulips add movement to a quiet tabletop composition.*
Overleaf, left: *Cream anemones and pink jasmine complement the room's rosy interior.*
Overleaf, right: *Speckled fritillarias and violets are the perfect counterpoint to cut crystal vases.*

"Perfumes are the feelings of flowers."

—Heinrich Heine, poet

Right: *A refreshing and stylish arrangement of clematis, porcelain berries, hydrangea, honeysuckle and Cosmos welcomes guests.* **Overleaf:** *Orange inflorescences, yellow tomatoes, dill and kangaroo paws add zest to glaucous and lilac hues.*

Gone with the Wind, Scarlett O'Hara descends the grand staircase of Tara, the walls behind her graced with a pink-striped wallpaper adorned with boughs of hydrangea. And although radishes are all she could find in the garden after the ravages of the war took her family and her farm, she has been honored with a breed of morning glory named after her—the bright red blooms a reflection of either her hair color or her fiery hot temper. Whichever the case, her mystique lives on forever through flowers. And while average gardeners may not be immortalized with plants named after them, what grows in their garden is as much of a reflection of themselves as the clothes they wear. ¶ Nature's truly glamorous floral creations can, without question, transmit the same mystique as the stars fashioned by Hollywood's dream factories. There is the way in

Right: *A painted mural brings the outdoors inside. The exoticism of the scene and the intense palette of the flowers accentuates the room's lustrous glamour.* **Overleaf:** *Sunny yellow tree peonies echo an arrangement of Icelandic poppies, torch lilies and pink peonies in an antique Delft vase.*

which the Technicolor fantasy of exotic orchids or birds of paradise can enliven even the most innocuous space, instantly transforming a living room in Terre Haute or Tulsa into a tropical retreat. Or the way a mass of Dutch tulips can evoke a favorite garden in springtime even in the darkest days of winter. In other cases, a sophisticated arrangement takes on the qualities of the room it inhabits. For instance, in the way a colorful diptych of Matisse prints is complemented by a riotous arrangement of overscale branches of flowering cherry blossoms, or how carefully the intricate colors painted on a Chinoiserie cabinet are reflected in the grouping of tulips set atop it. ¶ As with other stylish endeavors such as fashion design and interior design, trends, even fads, erupt and subside in floral design. But truly glamorous arrangements often

Right: *Overscale cherry tree blossoms flank a pair of Matisse prints.*
Overleaf, left: *The elongated lines of the calla lily stems complement the sensuous curves of the chair.*
Overleaf, right: *Glittering Murano glass contains freesia and sweet peas.*

hearken back to the same essential attributes of any classically designed room: order, symmetry and balance. Like the rooms they often live in, glamorous floral designs needn't be formal and fussy, or possess pretentions to occupy staid, museum-like spaces. Rather, they need only hew to those principles of scale and proportion of any beautifully designed space. What could be more elegant—or stately—than a simple clutch of tulips magnified in elegance by doubling the arrangement? Or what could be more sophisticated than branches of flowering blossoms profusely grouped in a porcelain vase, dominating an equally stylish space? ¶ Just as in film, when it comes to floral designs for interiors, it is the stage setting that can elevate them even more. Sometimes this is achieved merely by the choice of container. The simple repurposing of an antique

Right: *Overscale branches anchor an elegant space.* **Overleaf:** *Ephemeral spring greens— viburnum and hellebore—and creamy whites—ranunculus, roses, gardenias and Phalaenopsis orchids— gently echo the Venetian vessels. Tulips and a chartreuse cymbidium orchid animate the scene.*

porcelain cachepot as a receptacle for an unruly bunch of dogwood branches transforms their wild blossoms into an elegant domestic arrangement. Similarly, the formality of a glinting crystal vase can be dressed down by the profusion of sweet pea blossoms it contains, or its pedigree further enhanced by the inclusion of a tightly structured bouquet of mixed blooms. Individual flowers, like individual actors, have distinct personalities. The way they come together as a cast—or arrangement—or conduct a solo performance has a profound effect on the space they occupy, and the emotions they incite in us, the audience. ¶ Like an actor on the stage, some individuals among us lead lives so dramatic—as brightly lit and extravagantly colored as the most outlandish bouquet—that their influence is indelible. One such force was Diana Vreeland, the

Right: *Boughs of rhododendron add an unexpected touch to a sparkling foyer.*
Overleaf: *Floral art imitates life in porcelain and furniture.*

fabled editor of *Vogue* magazine from 1962 to 1971. Vreeland loved flowers, and she loved the color red. Vreeland was "discovered" by *Harper's Bazaar* editor in chief Carmel Snow when she spotted her at the St. Regis Hotel in New York dancing in a white lace dress, her hair adorned with white roses. Snow promptly hired her. ¶ Years later, Vreeland—as grand and exotic as any of the fashion shoots she directed—hired famed decorator Billy Baldwin to decorate her Park Avenue apartment, stating that she wanted her living room to "look like a garden, but a garden in hell." The result: red everything; furniture and walls covered in floral chintzes, floral motif accents everywhere, and tables covered with large floral bouquets and windowsills filled with large pots of lilies and amaryllis. As Vreeland once summarized, "another vase of

Left: *The graphic impact of black, white and red is illustrated in this bold composition of anemone, carnations, tulips and roses.*

flowers on the table doesn't bother me if the flowers are divine." ¶ The power of a rose is as undeniable as the power of red, a color that Vreeland once described as "the great clarifier—bright, cleansing, and revealing. I can't imagine becoming bored with red—it would be like becoming bored with the person you love." Roses are magnetic, like the most stimulating individuals: they are powerful, passionate, titillating and for centuries the iconic symbol of passion and love. For this reason, they are given in profusion on Valentine's Day. Artists of all disciplines, including writers, filmmakers, and particularly musicians, have been drawn to the rose for centuries, owing to its symbolism as a metaphor for the sensual and sexual. In music, the subject encompasses all genres, crossing boundaries from cabaret to country, and classical to

Right: *A 19th-century glazed Italian ceramic pot is filled with Leonardo da Vinci roses.*

rock—from the 1800s ballad "The Yellow Rose of Texas," and French cabaret star Édith Piaf's moody "La Vie en Rose" in the 1940s, to country music star Lynn Anderson's signature song "I Never Promised You a Rose Garden" and Marie Osmond's "Paper Roses," from 1971 and 1973, respectively. Bette Midler's robust rendition of "The Rose" was a megahit in 1979, claiming the number 3 spot on *Billboard* magazine's Hot 100 list for the year. There is no denying the endless fount of inspiration the rose has proven to be for musicians and recording artists over the decades. ¶ While there are thousands and thousands of songs about roses going back hundreds of years—lore has it the number may be as high as four thousand—the mention of a rose in a lyric isn't always, or often, about the plant itself. The rose often serves as a

Left: *Passionflower vine adds an exotic note to a romantic arrangement of fresh cut roses.*

"God gave us memory so that we might have roses in December."

—James Matthew Barrie, author

symbol of unrequited love, or even heartbreak. Similarly, in literature, the rose is often a bittersweet symbol. In Emily Brontë's "A Little Budding Rose," the poet also compares the rose to love, but to a broken one:

The rose is blasted, withered, blighted,
Its root has felt a worm,
And like a heart beloved and slighted,
Failed, faded, shrunk its form.

And of course in Shakespeare's *Romeo and Juliet*, one of the tragic lovers speaks the phrase, "A rose by any other name would smell as sweet." ¶ Finally, the visual symbolism of red in film has exerted a powerful influence—think of Doro-

Right: *Roses, unadorned, are the height of sophistication.*
Overleaf: *Roses of any shade add glamour to any arrangement.*

MARIO TESTINO PORTRAITS

thy's ruby slippers and the deadly scarlet poppies she falls asleep upon. From *The Black Rose*, in 1950, to *The White Rose* in 1982, to the iconic scene in Sam Mendes's 1999 classic *American Beauty*, in which actress Mena Suvari basks naked in a sea of the signature rose, this iconic flower has played a leading role in shaping our celluloid fantasies. What could be more glamorous?

Left: *Fuchsia and hot-pink blossoms are unapologetically electric.* **Overleaf:** *Tulips, figs, hyacinth and roses fill a 19th-century English quill basket set atop an antique Italian table.*

"The Amen!
of Nature
is always
a flower."

—Oliver Wendell Holmes, poet

Right: *Candy-colored parrot tulips are theatrical and timeless.*

"When in doubt, wear Red."

— Bill Blass, fashion designer

Powerful, strong, energizing. Red is all of those things—and more. It's the color of love. Just think of the symbolism that a simple red rose conveys, much less a dozen. There's passion and beauty and desire wrapped up in red, but also honor and confidence. There's Chinese red, a symbol of good luck and prosperity. Red is snappy, but it's also serious. Fire trucks, warning signs and emergency services all convey urgency through the color. Tastemakers even claim that no room or outfit is complete without a touch of red, be it the lining of a lampshade or a touch of rouge lipstick. The color is sumptuous (think red velvet walls), and indulgent (hello, red velvet cupcakes). It's also invigorating: think the sweet yet bitter taste of Campari on ice cooling on the hottest of summer days. When working with red flowers, you're not mincing your words or your thoughts. Bouquets of any red flower, from poppies to parrot tulips, make a decisive statement—one that's unapologetic and unforgettable. That's the power of red.

Fig.1.ª

b

1.ᶜ

1.ᶠ

1.ᵍ

1.ᵉ

4.ᵉ

4.ᵇ

2.ʰ

2.ⁱ

3.ᵉ

3.ª Fig.3.ª

3.ᵇ

Fig.4

a

Fig.6.ª

4.ᶠ

6.ᵇ

Fig.9

9.ᶜ

9.ª

4.ᶜ

Fig.8.ª

Fig. 3.d

Fig. 11.

Fig. 7.

Bold
Beautiful
Exuberant

"I always notice flowers."

—Andy Warhol, artist

Right: *A bountiful arrangement of camellia branches and Hawaiian orchids is accompanied by clusters of garden roses, amaryllis and a cascade of oranges. Pomegranates and castor bean pods rest on the platter below.*

98

Do you always notice flowers? What is your first flower memory? Was it seeing an allée of cherry blossoms budding for the first time? A table set for Sunday supper, adorned with fresh wildflowers picked from the roadside? Do you remember the first time you realized flowers emanated a scent? Maybe it was the sweet smell of a gardenia that tickled your nose (hopefully, it wasn't anything pungent). Or maybe you remember the impact of an imposing public display of flowers. Flowers at their simplest always make a statement, affecting the quality of the space they occupy and those of us who occupy those spaces.

Right: *Even without flowers, a grouping of massive magnolia branches creates a sculptural focal point.*
Overleaf: *It takes bold pink peonies to stand up to a room filled with pattern and color.*

But often it is the grandeur of the arrangement that affects us most, a power often achieved by a sense of scale. These compositions are larger than life, possess a rich lushness defined through a profusion of color (or even just texture), and convey an intoxicating joie de vivre—and an undeniable sense of celebration. ¶ The fantastically overscale designs that welcome guests to the Great Hall of the Metropolitan Museum of Art in New York have captivated visitors' attention for years, rivaling the finest sculptures and paintings in the museum for their ability to dazzle. *Reader's Digest* cofounder Lila Acheson Wallace established a permanent fund for fresh flowers in the hall after its renovation in 1969. Since then, there have been only two floral designers for these magnificent arrangements (which are generally ten to twelve feet tall): Chris Giftos, who held the post for thirty-three years (and

Right: *Virginia creeper and wild rose hips form an ethereal crown that wends gracefully around a 19th-century bust.*
Overleaf: *Large crimson peonies add a bold verve to an exotic living room.*

designed the bouquet of yellow freesia Elizabeth Taylor carried during her first marriage to Richard Burton, an arrangement so spectacular it flew on its own airline seat to get to the wedding), and his onetime apprentice, Remco van Vliet, who has fashioned the dramatic scenarios since 2003. In so many places, flowers actually come to define the space, acting as an indelible signature. Take the celebrated French restaurant La Grenouille in New York, for instance. Although it is Michelin starred and one of the most famous restaurants in the world, it is equally renowned for its lavish floral arrangements, to which an entire book—not a cookbook—has been dedicated. Of course, creating a perfectly sumptuous floral arrangement may require as many steps and ingredients as the most complicated French recipe. With floral design, as with gastronomy, certain elements

Right: *Dendrobium orchids, ferns and horsetail bamboo rest in an otherworldly mossy container.*

"Every flower is a soul opening out into nature."

—Gérard de Nerval, poet

Left: *Tree branches, fruits, vines and vegetables emphasize the scale of a pair of rough-hewn vessels.*

just shouldn't work together in theory, but in the hands of a master chef or great designer, nuance can be extracted from seeming discord, elevating each individual ingredient to a higher plane, while creating a spectacularly harmonious dish or composition. ¶ Sometimes the hallmarks of a great creation are bold and exuberant, possessing stronger notes and a powerful finish; at other times, it is the subtlety of the mix and delicacy of the textures that tell the story, yet still create a powerful wow factor. These qualities are especially true when it comes to floral arrangements. For instance, giant rambling branches juxtaposed with tiny petaled plants or wild, unwieldy vines matched with delicately pointed fronds. Perhaps fruits and flowers combined into a solo arrangement. And while boldness cannot be confined to or defined by any particular color, certain arrangements such as those that combine deep

*Left: A tight composition of deep maroon dahlias, yarrow and coneflower heads anchor the centerpiece, while elongated green amaranth cascades down. **Overleaf:** Fruits and vegetables transform a lush floral arrangement into a veritable cornucopia of style.*

and vibrant pink, robust purples and aubergines, or ravishing reds create an impact that's difficult to miss. Although most often created in autumn or around the holidays, these compositions are delightful year-round. ¶ To call a flower bold is not to say it is brassy; to pronounce a flower beautiful is not to call it excessive; and to describe a flower as exuberant is not to claim it is overly assertive, but rather simply joyful. All of these confident phrases can be applied to flowers and arrangements that are at once in your face for the way they command attention, but at the same time appear tasteful and well considered. Sometimes simplicity can be bold. And who knew how to play that hand more deftly than some of the great hostesses and social leaders who have captured our attention over the years with their own attention to the power of flowers to signify sta-

Right: *Dutch hydrangea, scented geraniums, agapanthus seed pods and Ligustrum berries impart a pleasing complexity.*

The socialite also hired renowned British garden designer Russell Page to transform the gardens at her country home in Long Island, Kiluna Farm, where the team planted bountiful beds of azaleas, rhododendrons, dogwoods, and tulip poplars. Paley's friend and social doyenne C. Z. Guest was also a passionate gardener who gained authority later in life for her books on the subject. Guest once remarked, "I've always felt that having a garden is like having a good and loyal friend." Similarly, Rachel "Bunny" Mellon was a leading social force as well as a generous philanthropist, passionate art collector and self-trained authority on American horticulture. Among the many gardens she designed, perhaps none is so prominent as the White House Rose Garden. Both Guest and Mellon were—like certain flowers—known for their restraint, while

Left: *An elegant tabletop composition represents the mood and feeling of a Dutch still life.*
Overleaf: *Freshly cut flowers and floral prints make the bedroom a restful haven.*

"It's spring and everyone's in love and flowers pick themselves."

—e. e. cummings, poet

Walpole
Cedar Products
WALPOLE WOODWORKERS, INC.
WALPOLE, MASSACHUSETTS
1-800-394-1932

other social dynamos exhibited a bolder appetite in their ardor for flowers in every form. Nan Kempner, the New York socialite often credited as the model for Tom Wolfe's description in his novel *Bonfire of the Vanities* of the "social X-ray": a woman who could never be "too rich or too thin," displayed her passion for flowers in her dress, lifestyle, and decor. In a fitting tribute she and her husband's fiftieth wedding anniversary was held in 2002 at New York's Botanical Gardens. The two directives on the invitation read: "Black tie. Please wear flowers." Carolyne Roehm, Kemper's friend and a noted author and expert on flowers as well, wore a gown with sleeves made of gardenias. ¶ But whether on a dress or a desk or a dresser, flowers are used to capture daydreams and fantasies in wildly imaginative ways to take people away from their everyday lives, transporting them to another world. And for that, no RSVP or invitation is ever required.

Right: Tiny yellow-faced flowers mirror the tones of big blooms in this bouquet of mock orange blossoms, roses and dicentra foliage. **Overleaf:** *Flowers are combined with fresh fruit, in a similar shade, to create a look that is as colorful as the antique bench upon which they reside.*

"It is at the edge of the petal that love waits."

—William Carlos Williams, poet

Right: *Yellow and white peonies, garden rose, scabiosa, honeysuckle vine, lilac, dogwood and cherry branches make up a grand composition.* **Overleaf:** *Wild Italian white sweet peas seemingly explode from a 19th-century cast iron urn.*

140

"I believe in

Pink."

–Audrey Hepburn, actress

Pink is a happy color. Pink flowers flirt without seducing; they tease without taunting. From cherry blossoms and peonies to tulips and poppies, pink is powerful. Bruce Springsteen and Aretha Franklin both channeled the color, singing about driving a pink Cadillac. But traveling to certain locales doesn't require rose-colored glasses. The Indian city of Jaipur is known as the Pink City; Petra, Jordan, is known as the Rose City; then there's Marrakesh, which is known as the Pink City, the Rose City and the Red City. And despite the hustle and bustle of these places, pink can be a nurturing color. It signifies hope, and it's the color of romance. Softer shades are calming, while more vibrant hues excite and tantalize (without the harshness of red). Yet all pinks are not the same. Certain signature shades are as identifiable as any corporate logo: cotton candy, Mary Kay cosmetics, grapefruit, the pink ribbon, bubble gum—even Pepto-Bismol. It's the nuance of pink that takes it from sweet to chic. And if you doubt pink's influence, just think about the irresistible allure of a pink French macaroon or a single magenta gerbera daisy. Few things are as sublime.

Fig. 1.

1.ª

13.ᵍ

3.ᶜ

3.ᵇ   3.ᵈ

5.ᶜ

a

6.ᵉ

Fig. 3.

6.ᶠ

1.ᶜ

4.

9.ᶜ

9.ᵍ

Fig. 9.

6.ᶠ

Fig. 2.

10.ᵈ

10.ᶜ

10.ᶠ

12.ᶜ

b   a

4.ᵒ

9.ᵇ

9.ᶜ

F.1

10.ᵉ

12.ᵈ

perhaps magically even smell it, when seeing evocative pictures of that oasis of calm. Or consider the wildly eccentric gardens of Lotusland near Santa Barbara, California with, among others, their topiary, water, fern, cactus and bromeliad gardens, each of which is spellbinding in its ability to transport the mind. These special spaces are both tangible and real, elusive and imaginary. No matter how exotic, foreign or faraway, we can be transported there by our shared understanding of the flower's uncanny ability to transform feelings and emotions. ¶ Today, we share in common a certain "language of flowers," a simple discourse that is understood almost universally. Most anyone, virtually anywhere, can have fresh flowers, simple blossoms picked either from the garden or the roadside, or elaborate bouquets ordered up from a fine florist. Such a state

Left: *Roses, columbines and sweet peas gather in an Empire painted tole egg conserver.*

of democracy has not always been the case, though, and indeed certain rare specimens, such as the so-called ghost orchid, the search for which inspired Susan Orlean's spellbinding read, *The Orchid Thief*, can command unimaginable sums, and drive individuals to unimaginable acts to possess them. Indeed, in 1633, a farmhouse in Hoorn, the Netherlands, was exchanged for three rare tulip bulbs at the beginning of Tulipomania, which seized that country in the 17th century. Of course the mania for flowers is truly a passion that has influenced the evolution of world cultures since the beginning of time, inspiring artists, writers, designers, architects and great thinkers in the production of their finest works. One of the greatest flourishings of this confluence is found in the Golden Age of floral still-life painting that emerged in the northern countries in the 16th

Left: *Black grapes and chestnut seeds spill onto a cloth, bringing unusual elements to an evocative tabletop arrangement of crimson garden roses and andromeda.*

and 17th centuries. ¶ The genre of floral still-life painting coincided with an explosion of interest in the natural world and the creation of lavish botanical encyclopedias recording the discoveries of the New World and Asia. Natural objects, and flowers in particular, began to be appreciated as individual items worthy of study and appreciation, apart from their religious and mythological associations. Many of the great floral still lifes of the period are actually fantasias that the artist created by consulting these herbal and botanical texts, combining flowers from different countries and continents in impossible groupings of eccentric bouquets. ¶ This compositional form—exotic, erotic, alluring and magical—dominated the visual and design discourse for another century, and it was only in the mid-19th century that a true "language of flowers" began to be expressed

Right: *A delicate butterfly, artfully placed, completes a "still life" of peonies and fritillarias.*

poetically and linguistically in the Victorian era, when a new culture of flowers as a pure form of communication and decoration arose. For lovers and others whose emotions were stifled by social strictures of propriety imposed on an already restrained society, the exoticism, elusiveness and not so subtle sexuality of floral blooms became a perfect vehicle for communicating more than mere words could (or should) allow.

¶ Perhaps it should not be surprising that it took a child of the Victorian era, Constance Spry, to revolutionize the art of floral arrangement. Like others, inspired by 17th century Dutch flower paintings and her own growing collection of 18th- and 19th-century flower books, Spry took a decidedly more democratic approach to the art of arranging flowers, one she advocated when she opened her first shop in London,

Left: *Berry-colored dahlias, scabiosa, amaranths, celosia, porcelain berries and hydrangea have a painterly palette.*

Flower Decorations, in 1929. Convinced that one's imagination should not be confined by a limited budget, she championed affordable resources, asymmetry in composition, and the use of humble materials: flowers plucked from the hedgerow; plants others might consider weeds; twigs, logs and other plant matter not usually selected for "fine" arrangements; and containers recycled from the kitchen cupboard or storage barn. Spry thought nothing of combining kale leaves and roses and presenting them in pickle and jam jars, or humble pieces of crockery. Her arrangements, though elegant and sophisticated—her clients included Cecil Beaton and Wallis Simpson— also set a tone for floral arrangements that would be as at home in privileged drawing rooms of mid-20th-century London and Paris as they would be in shabby-chic American interiors of

Right: Delicate blossoms and leafy textures of ranunculus, garden roses, oregano, honeysuckle and euphorbia offset the sharp geometry of angular succulents.

today. Of course, each country has a floral language that is uniquely its own, and visual idioms that are indebted to the dominance of that language—the patterns and tones of its national flowers. For instance, if there were ever a national fabric, France would claim the toile de Jouy (patterned fabrics with pastoral scenes). Similarly, the English can claim chintz. Chintz fabrics, which are glazed cottons often emblazoned with large floral prints, have long been associated with grand English country houses of the late 19th and early 20th centuries. Floral chintzes often feature "old-fashioned" flowers such as hollyhock, hydrangea, roses, lilacs and bountiful bouquets with ribbons, vines, tendrils and, sometimes, animals. With a subtle sheen, they usually served as slipcovers (often until threadbare), as well as window treatments. ¶ In the 1930s,

Left: Old-fashioned flowers—and fruits—are represented in this composition of peaches, blackberries, black basil, coleus, artemisia, garden roses, sea oat grass and globe amaranth.

pioneering American designer Dorothy Draper used them in projects such as the Greenbrier resort, with its chartreuse and hot-pink motifs. She even created a gutsy rhododendron-patterned fabric that is still in production today. Floral chintzes had a long and popular run until their overuse in the 1980s when a bedroom, for example, might contain a single chintz covering everything from skirted tables, balloon shades and canopy beds to duvets, bed skirts, lampshades and even upholstery on the walls. The overworked motif practically disappeared in the 1990s, and only resurfaced more than a decade later in newly reincarnated forms. Floral prints were now over-scaled, their patterns simplified, their color palettes updated; even old document prints were reworked and revitalized for contemporary audiences. Chintz was back, finding a new, hip

Right: *A mix of garden-variety pansies and clematis pair well with a rustic cement cachepot. The wooden chair is 19th-century Austrian.*

21st-century audience: now you are just as likely to find chintz patterns in a contemporary downtown loft as a Neo-Georgian suburban estate. ¶ Like the untamed patterns in these newer fabrics, the flowers in today's simpler designs feel less contrived—or completely uncontrived. Compositions of wildflowers, bark, branches and even mounds of moss have found their way into the most formal of spaces. Gone are the days of arrangements containing filler of baby's breath or throwaway hothouse botanicals. Today, arrangements are more thoughtful, reminiscent of Victorian-era designs. Nosegays, which are also called posies or tussie-mussies, are petite arrangements where every flower has a special meaning—a sort of sign language of flowers. These miniature designs, a little larger than a boutonniere were popular gifts of the Victorian era. Made up

Left: *A twig-wrapped vase was created with as much thought as the plants it holds: roses, pinecones, ferns and purple ti leaves.*

of flowers and herbs, they often contained complicated messages, hence their other moniker, "the talking bouquets." Today, while the act of handcrafting and giving nosegays hasn't captured the attention of a broader audience just yet, more thought is certainly being given to the meaning of each flower that is chosen for an arrangement, particularly when given as a gift. To thank a dear friend for a birthday present you received, an arrangement might include a mix of ivy (friendship), honey-suckle (devotion and affection), marjoram (for joy and kindness) and hydrangea (to convey appreciation). Or to send someone condolences, a combination of balm (sympathy), purple hyacinth (sorrow), morning glory (affection), rosemary (remembrance) and white poppy (consolation) will offer solace. A flirtation can be conveyed with a

Right: *The meaning of tulips? White: forgiveness. Yellow: good cheer. Pink: affection, but not as romantic as red.* **Overleaf:** *A parterre garden of salmon-colored and white roses echoes an interior palette with the same soft, soothing shades.*

posy of ranunculus, which is much more direct, translating to "I am dazzled by your charms." ¶ The charm that comes from knowing the language of flowers allows you to create and send thoughtful arrangements that are not only coveted for their beauty, but also cherished for the extra special thought put into each selection. Besides a monogrammed present, few things could be more personal. ¶ That said, don't feel the need to overanalyze the flowers you're giving—or receiving, for that matter. At the very least, a gathering of blooms or burst of color is a warm welcome in almost anyone's life—no translation needed.

Left: *Succulents, purple basil, Chocolate Cosmos, Muscari, and garden roses make a richly colored arrangement.*
Overleaf: *Marigolds, copper beech leaves, golden amaranth and irises echo a deeply saturated— and emotive—Johannes Vermeer painting.*

"Where flowers bloom, so does hope."

—Lady Bird Johnson, first lady and conservationist

Right: *A bounty of fresh-cut flowers in fiery tones.*

Overleaf: *Maidenhair fern, spray roses and white peonies complete the table setting for an elegant luncheon.*

182

"It's always best to start at the beginning— and all you do is follow the Yellow Brick Road."

—Glinda the Good Witch, *The Wizard of Oz*

Everything is better at the end of the Yellow Brick Road. It's no coincidence that yellow is so often chosen for those looking for hope, need cheering up or are recovering from an illness. The color is sunny and optimistic. When Kate Middleton, the Duchess of Cambridge, was released from the hospital after a short stay for a serious bout of morning sickness, she was carrying a bouquet of yellow flowers. The scene was captured by throngs of photographers, while tabloid reporters examined the symbolism of the color: was the child to be named Dandelion? (She was carrying roses.) Was she having a boy or a girl? Perhaps yellow was to be the neutral paint color of the nursery of the baby whose sex was yet to be determined. Of course, reporters also questioned the significance of the hue of the baby-blue scarf she was also wearing that day. Assumptions aside, the yellow flowers seem to have been prescribed simply as a dose of good cheer. The smell of freshly cut citrus, especially lemons, evokes daydreams of basking in warm rays of Florida sunshine. Yet beyond yellow's always sunny outlook, the color can evoke images of gold and wealth and riches.

Fig.1.

Fig.11.

Fig.4.

Fig.14.

Fig.15.

Contemporary Chic Cosmopolitan

"*Simplicity is the law of nature for men as well as for flowers.*"

—Henry David Thoreau, author

Right: *A simple mass of moss reflects the same angular lines of the table and artwork above it.*

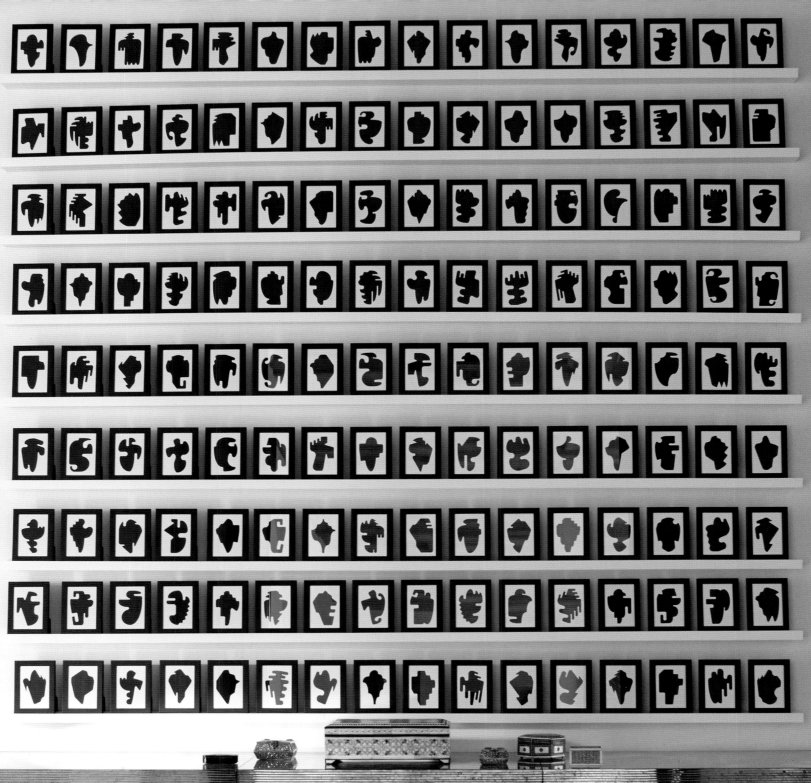

Can a plant or flower that has lived on this planet for thousands of years be considered modern, or truly contemporary? The answer is unequivocally yes. For instance, what could be more timeless, yet at the same time classic *and* contemporary, than the water lily? This simple and elegant specimen has been found to be one of two of the earliest types of flowering plants to appear on Earth. Although the water lily doesn't often appear in domestic arrangements due to its great delicacy, other flowers that have been around for millennia can seem somehow utterly fresh

Right: *A tall vase of tropical fronds adds a natural touch to a space that feels like a cloud.*
Overleaf: *Red calla lilies and dahlias—seemingly dancing across the table—make a robust statement in a chic dining room.*

194

and contemporary, whereas others can feel dated or defined by the strictures of the time in which they were first popularized. ¶ Take the calla lily, for instance, with its elongated stem as long and chic as a stiletto heel. What could feel more contemporary? Their fluid, languid stems capped by sensually unfurling blossoms make these a go-to sexy flower time and time again. And almost always, calla lilies are used unaccompanied, individually or in groups to create arrangements that feel particularly cosmopolitan in their architectonic structure and ultrasophisticated in their self-possession. Anemones are another contemporary favorite. Grown in a veritable rainbow of colors, each flower, regardless of hue, features a large black center looking like nothing so much as the bull's-eye on a target, or the infinite pupil of the human eye. ¶ "Contemporary

Left: *A collection of anemones is the perfect match for a black-and-white dining room.*

flowers" may sound like an oxymoron, but in an interesting paradox, many flowers somehow appear even more modern when they are placed in traditional or historic interiors. The Four Seasons Hotel George V in Paris, housed in a formerly private 19th-century residence in the eighth arrondissement, has become a Valhalla of sorts for those on a pilgrimage to see truly cutting-edge floral design. The avant-garde arrangements that Jeff Leatham has been creating since 1999 for this hallowed establishment have developed a cultlike following as they exert an unimaginable influence on trends in floral design internationally. While his creations would be just as spectacular if displayed in a modern white box, the somewhat jarring juxtaposition of his radically new designs in an otherwise classic and formal environment gives them that extra verve,

Right: *Dried Cecropia leaves draw upon the same palette as the room they inhabit, giving the entire space the feeling of a sepia photograph.*

perhaps making them even more successful. ¶ The right contemporary arrangement is as important as any lone accessory, whether it's the perfect wrist cuff to complete an ensemble, or the indispensable side table that completes a room. And like any essential accessory, the right flower or floral arrangement becomes sculpture in its own right, lending the extra visual punch necessary to energize a room, transforming a routine or already beautiful space into somewhere that's more exciting and perhaps a little dazzling. And as with any great object, the perfect floral statement doesn't have to be exotic or esoteric to be seriously chic. ¶ Even the modest carnation—which some might consider a bit too common to be exceptional—is one of the easiest if most unexpected flowers to make contemporary. Grouped en masse, the flowers can be striking and daring,

Left: *A simple vase of tulips serves as the lone accessory in a clean-lined space.* **Overleaf:** *A giant bough of eucalyptus is treated as sculpture in a room filled with antiques, contemporary art and exquisite architectural detailing.*

demonstrating both fearlessness and confidence. As with any design conundrum, creating successful contemporary floral designs relies on several simple principles such as emphasizing strong, elongated lines; restricting oneself to a limited, well-defined palette; and knowing when to judiciously edit or generously mass a singular material. Contemporary arrangements are also the perfect way to flirt with color for those who tend toward neutral palettes. Rooms painted in bold, bright colors aren't for everyone, and that is why petite arrangements are great ways to incorporate unexpected color into a space without a long-term commitment. ¶ Coco Chanel once famously stated that "elegance is refusal," and so it is when it comes to the design of strikingly contemporary floral designs that are as timeless and chic as a Chanel suit. Perhaps it is not surprising

Left: *A little pop of purple adds a dash of personality to an all-white space without overpowering it.*
Overleaf: *Assertive and spiky yellow blooms are colorful and sculptural additions to their respective spaces.*

that fashion and flowers have always been intertwined. In the entrancing documentary *Ultrasuede*, which chronicles the life and, often, excessive times of fashion designer Halston in the era of Studio 54, one of the jaw-dropping moments of the film comes when it is revealed that in the early 1980s he spent in the low six figures annually for white orchids—just for the offices! ¶ Elsa Schiaparelli, who is sometimes credited with inventing modern women's fashion, was known for her embroideries and hats featuring dazzling floral confections. As a child, she planted flower seeds in her mouth and ears, seriously hoping that they would grow into a garden and beautify her face. Recalling that memory as an adult, she created a blue cotton summer dress featuring appliquéd prints of flower-seed packets. She also joined forces with surrealist artists Salvador

Right: *Exotic tropicals add an organic touch to a streamlined space.*
Overleaf, left: *A bough of Japanese maple branches echoes the pared-down aesthetic of the room.*
Overleaf, right: *Magnolias float in a pool of water lilies.*

"If you find cut flowers too extravagant, stick to the greens."

—Dorothy Draper, designer

Right: *Mosses and bromeliads create a delicate microenvironment.*
Overleaf: *A bold massing of magnolia branches balances a perfectly composed interior.*

Dalí and Jean Cocteau, and she and Cocteau famously collaborated on an evening coat that featured a double image of lovers kissing below a vase of pink roses. These larger-than-life creations attracted larger-than-life personalities, including Mae West, as customers. ¶ In 1947, when Christian Dior debuted his famous New Look collection after World War II, he had his salon at 30 Avenue Montaigne strewn with flowers by Lachaume, the Parisian floral house that was founded in 1845 (and which is also where Marcel Proust went daily to purchase the signature fresh cattleya that would decorate his buttonhole). In Dior's new introductions, he signaled that change was ahead—he wanted to reintroduce women to their feminine curves after years of rationing and uniforms. And even now, decades later, the company channels that

Left: A fiery vase of crimson orchids offers the same verve as the cutting-edge artwork behind it.
Overleaf: Pink peonies feature the same visual punch as the yellow room they inhabit.

gung-ho spirit into a fragrance—called New Look—which it describes as an "explosion of flowers, generous, opulent and ultrafeminine." In 2012, the fashion house's designer Raf Simons hearkened to Dior in 1947 by commissioning Paris florist Eric Chauvin to cover the walls of five different rooms within a hôtel particulier until they were completely enveloped with blooms. One of the most memorable was a room covered with blue delphiniums, almost electric in their hue. With one million flowers used, Simons said the flowers were a metaphor for the collection as a whole, which treaded between the past and the future. ¶ Early on, Coco Chanel claimed the camellia as her signature flower, in turn making it her house symbol. Karl Lagerfeld continues the tradition to this day at Chanel, incorporating the floral motif into quilted

Right: *Three simple dahlias are perfectly shaped for tall, laboratory-style vases.*
Overleaf: *Glinting colored vases are filled with exotic calla lilies and orchids.*

jackets and handbags with dangly gold chains. Mary Quant would pick up on the interest of flower power in swinging 1960s London, where she reigned as the fashion designer of Britain's hip set. And even Yves Saint Laurent, in his couture, ready-to-wear, and Rive Gauche collections flaunted his love of flowers. Today, Valentino emblazons giant appliqué flowers on billowing gowns, and Moschino has revived quirky floral prints, including them on everything from embroidered organza drop-waist dresses to rose-shaped satin handbags. ¶ In the United States, perhaps no designer is as linked to flowers as Oscar de le Renta. His Connecticut estate, with perfectly trimmed boxwood parterres, is a standard-bearer of fine garden design. And his oasis in the Dominican Republic seamlessly blends indoors and out. That sensitive connection

Left: *Branches from the garden add softness to a room without overpowering the space.*
Overleaf: *Bold colors set in black vessels and vases strike an effortlessly chic note.*

to nature works its way into de la Renta's numerous home decor and fashion collections through frilly flower-laden dresses and exotic Indian-inspired tree-of-life fabrics, as well as dinner plates and accessories featuring historic floral and botanical images he selected from the archives of the New York Botanical Garden. But at the hands of de la Renta, the centuries-old flower patterns felt of the moment, new and forward-thinking. ¶ With fashion, as with flowers, knowing the past and building upon it, but not repeating it, is what makes something truly modern—and daring.

Right: *To make an arrangement seem contemporary, play with scale. A petite composition of peonies completes a still life.* **Overleaf:** *Conversely, an overscale vase of blooming branches adds drama to a bedroom.*

"I must have flowers, always, and always."

—Claude Monet, artist

Right: *Sweet peas are elegant in their simplicity.*
Overleaf: *The arching sweep of yellow calla lilies echoes the chic lines of a modern interior.*

"White . . . . is not a mere absence of color; it is a shining and affirmative thing, as fierce as red, as definite as black."

—Gilbert Keith Chesterton, author

White. Does any color say contemporary, chic, cosmopolitan, with more authority than white? Although it is perhaps the most universal of all colors—white is the union of all colors of the spectrum; black is the absence of color—white always feels particularly modern and assertively "now." From the radicalism of what is acknowledged to be the first white painting, Russian artist Kazimir Malevich's *Suprematist Composition: White on White*, 1918, to Le Corbusier's transformative modern architecture rendered in white and Elsie de Wolfe's refreshing white interiors, the color has since the early 20th century signaled renewal, freshness, clarity and order. Whether it be an immaculate arrangement of white roses as a centerpiece, a group of paper whites bursting forth from a terra-cotta planter in a windowsill or an elegant clutch of white tulips spilling generously from a sleek glass container, white flowers complete any interior. They lend a note of modernity to even the most classical space as well as a crisp elegance that balances the purity and perfection of the most modern space.

Fig. 10.

10.d

10.g

7.d

7.e

7.k

7.b

7.f

Fig. 7.

a

12.d

7.i

10.b

10.c

10.e

11.d

Fig. 3.

a

3.

a

Fig. 11.

4.g

4.c

4.e

Fig. 4.

8.b

Fig. 8.

8.c

a

Simple
Honest
Effortless

"Weeds are flowers too, once you get to know them."

—A. A. Milne, author

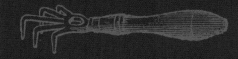

Right: *Angular quince branches echo the simple shapes and silhouettes of antique furnishings.*

Laudato si, Misignore
da la quale nullu homo vive

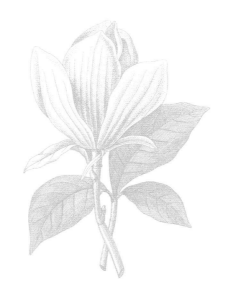

With each new millennium, and within each decade, we have witnessed the desire for a return to a simpler time. As technology accelerates, modes of communication proliferate, education improves and global awareness increases, we continue to see a collective desire to return to nature and slow things down. Of course, since the rise of the Roman Empire, "back to the land" movements have emerged in predictable cycles, whether it was defined by the writings of Emerson and Thoreau in the mid-19th century, or by the emergence of titles including the

Right: A creamy pitcher inspires a tendriled bouquet of poppies, peonies, garden roses, snapdragons, veronica, nasturtium and scented geraniums, which "pours" from its spout.

246

Mother Earth News and *Whole Earth Catalog* in the 1960s and today's sustainable movement led by chefs, farmers and writers like Dan Barber, Alice Waters and Michael Pollan. And if the slow food movement defined cultural trends in the first decade of the new millennium, today may ultimately be defined by the "rurbanistas," those with a passion for simplicity and authenticity who maintain one foot in the city and one in the country—or simply yearn to live a less complicated life. ¶ Just as with the culinary world's farm-to-table movement and trend toward foraging for the ultimate in locally sourced food, and the travel industry's shift toward ecotourism and responsible tourism, the floral community now has what some are calling the "petal to pedal" and "slow flower" movements. Both interests advocate the use of locally sourced flowers and organic

Left: *Black turnip roots complement Dutch sweet peas in a vase wrapped with bergenia leaves.*
Overleaf: *Dried botanicals grace a country farmhouse.*

gardening. With petal to pedal, the flowers will be picked and arranged—perhaps in a mason jar—and delivered to your door by bicycle. The slow flower movement is equally concerned about sourcing flowers domestically and locally, thereby reducing the carbon footprint of importing more exotic blooms from far-flung locales. Trends in floral design have also found their inspiration in these movements. For as striking as certain complicated arrangements might be, one could argue that nothing is more powerful and visually arresting than a simple roadside wildflower, its stem submerged in an old glass seltzer bottle. Modest floral designs are defined by the power of restraint. Today's garden, whether it is devoted to flowers, vegetables or, more commonly, both, is increasingly marked by the owner's attention to simple, organic principles and

Right: *Modest masses of pale hyacinths and roses underscore the understated elegance of the architecture.*
Overleaf: *Succulents and white florals—namely, anemone and ranunculus—combine in exquisite harmony.*

heirloom varietals. In the motion picture *It's Complicated*, Meryl Streep's character Jane toiled in a vegetable garden a *Los Angeles Times* blog described as "almost pornographic," in its "lushness, colorfulness, [and] perkiness." The garden in this film, splendid in its casual elegance, also served as a metaphor for seeking the path where love, like nature, was in fact less complicated. ¶ A deep regard for authenticity, and renewed interest in simpler values among floral and landscape designers and everyday gardeners, have accelerated exponentially in recent years. This aesthetic revival has prompted a commensurate growth in the marketplace for companies that specialize in heirloom seeds for both flowers and vegetables. People seem to long for the modest, seemingly once forgotten, sweet pea, primrose and daisy, among others. Nostalgia,

Right: *Lustrous white garden roses shine amid eucalyptus, wild rose hips and gentle, weeping andromeda.*
Overleaf: *Moroccan pottery displays clover, buttercup, orange calamondin, yellow and brown-eyed coreopsis, Forelle pears and Muscari.*

increasingly, is expressed in the garden. Cottage garden annuals such as moon-flower, four o'clocks, and forget-me-nots hearken to days gone by, a slower time and place. And one heirloom seed company, Seed Savers Exchange, a nonprofit organization dedicated to saving and sharing heirloom seeds, features eighteen varieties of sunflowers alone—eighteen! Those with a passion for horticulture seem increasingly inclined to take their cues from nature and its resources, rather than bending it to suit their will. Particularly in landscape design, we are witnessing a renaissance in restraint. From Oklahoma to California, where manicured, golf course–like landscaping once predominated, we see an increasing turn toward low-key, lower-maintenance materials with the use of heartier, drought-resistant native plants, natural grasses, and local wildflowers.

Left: *Tabletop bouquets composed of berries, anemones, ranunculus and carnations become individual still lifes under large antique cloches. They are surrounded by rambling vines of wild rose hips.*

This development has been christened as the "New Perennial" movement, and if the group has a leader, it is Dutch garden designer Piet Oudolf, perhaps best known for the creation of the High Line, an elevated freight rail line transformed into a public park on Manhattan's West Side. This prototypical example of the "wild nature" advocated by new perennialists features architectural plantings selected for their form, structure and hardiness rather than for their delicacy of color or elaborate design structure. ¶ While the less-is-more trend among horticulturalists has enjoyed an uptick in recent years, it has long been a mainstay among stylish designers. The legendary David Hicks, who is considered to be one of the most sophisticated contemporary designers of the 20th century, took a minimalist approach to floral arranging. The man perhaps best

Right: *A unique wood pitcher is home to an equally unusual arrangement of Asiatic lilies, calla lilies and begonia leaves.*

known for the uberchic, Coca-Cola-colored lacquer walls of his London living room, which inspired a generation of young designers, loved flowers so much he even published *The David Hicks Book of Flower Arranging* in 1976. As extravagant as his rooms may have been, he was not one to shy away from using the simplest objects as vessels to hold flowers. His advice: comb the hardware stores and kitchen departments for unexpected containers. Honey pots, soufflé dishes and jam jars were some of his eclectic go-tos. Even a common wastepaper basket was not beyond the realm of possibility for Hicks. He once placed a galvanized bucket with an arrangement of dried grasses, corn, sunflower and other seed heads atop an ornate 18th-century gilded console in a magnificent Park Avenue apartment. ¶ Sybil Connolly was another trailblazing fashion designer,

Left: *Delphiniums are a favorite of English cutting gardens and add a carefree spirit to elegant interiors.*

decorator and accomplished gardener who championed simple materials and celebrated her Irish heritage through her love of flowers and homespun crafts, such as basket weaving. As a fashion designer, Connolly was perhaps best known for creating couture from unassuming fabrics such as simple pleated Irish linen. But beyond fashion, she ventured into home design and gardening, which may have been where her heart lived. In the 1980s she coedited *In an Irish Garden* and created a collection called "Mrs. Delany's Flowers" for Tiffany & Co. This assortment of enameled clocks, decorative accessories and fine porcelain dinnerware was painted with simple, straightforward floral patterns including purplish-blue hydrangea; cool, jade green primrose; red geraniums and soft-pink roses, among others, each set against high-gloss black porcelain. ¶

Right: *Burro's tails cascade in silvery sartorial splendor below white dahlias and green chrysanthemums. The contrast of the weathered-terra-cotta pots is as important to the overall arrangements as the floral compositions.*

In addition, she created floral wallpapers and fabrics with Schumacher and Brunschwig & Fils, and even produced a mass-market bedding line, the patterns of which were inspired by her garden along Dublin's Merrion Square where she grew larkspur, tulips, honeysuckle, lilies of the valley, roses and ivy. The writer Arline Bleecker once referred to Connolly as "a combination of Julia Child, Laura Ashley, Martha Stewart and maybe even Mary Poppins, all rolled into one." Indeed, Connolly, with her various interests and influence, was a lifestyle brand before the term even existed. And at the root of her success, as is the case for many of the most talented designers and decorators, was a love of nature, plants and flowers with all their myriad variety and complexity, but at their essence, flowers that are simple, honest and effortless in their beauty.

Left: *A creamer full of backyard staples, including garden roses, oregano, lamb's ears, Angel Wing begonia and rudbeckia pods, conjures a sweet simplicity.*

"Earth laughs in flowers."

—Ralph Waldo Emerson, poet

Right: *A roughly hewn stone container provides a humble anchor to a simple arrangement.*

Is there anyone who doesn't love green? It is the defining color in nature and the source of nature's bounty: most every flower we know blossoms forth from a green plant. In Japan, green is regarded as the color of eternal life; universally, green is a recognized metaphor for fertility and prosperity. At the same time, green is the color of money and envy, but in its varied natural splendor, green suggests nothing so much as optimism, freshness, vitality and growth. The beauty of green pervades our environment: the grass beneath our feet, the evergreens that suggest the hope of spring even in the darkest winter, the herbs that sustain us and the succulents that inspire us by their resilience. Naturally green flowers can seem more rare to find, though hellebore, ranunculus, gladiolas and orchids are among the beautiful blooms we often find in the most striking arrangements. But it is their heartier and sturdier relatives—great dishes of succulents; carefully propagated fig, lemon, and lime trees; grand sprays of alocasia leaves or clusters of wild rose hips—that often compose dramatic statements that are at once deceptively simple, honest in their purity and seemingly effortless in their beauty.

"Green is the prime color of the world, and that from which its loveliness arises."

— Pedro Calderón de la Barca, dramatist

Fig. 14ᵃ
14ᵇ

Fig. 12
12
c

c
14
d   d

12ᵍ

12ʰ

12ᵉ   14ᶠ

Fig. 12ᵃ

14ᵉ

d
12

f
5

k   l   5
i   e

5ᵍ

a

a
5ʰ

Fig. 7.   a
7ᶜ

12ᶠ

1ᵇ

Fig. 5.
b
5ᵃ

Fig 5.

5·A

2ᶜ

1ᵃ

5
B

5ᶜ

Fig. 4ᵃ

Acknowledgments

SPECIAL THANKS to Luigi Menduni, Dayle Wood and Melissa Colgan for the talent, enthusiasm and expertise each of you brought to the project. My appreciation is heartfelt. To Aerin Lauder, for the thoughtful foreword. Also, Ari Notis, Cat Willett and Abby Wilson for your tireless efforts. To Jacqueline Deval, Chris Thompson, Scott Russo, Renee Yewdaev and Mary Hern for your creativity and passion for quality. To Jeffrey Grove, Barbara Howard and Marcia Sherrill for your unyielding support. And to my family, particularly my parents, Susan and Gaylord Smith; my sister, Leanna Smith Wood; and my grandparents, Betty and Calvin Foster and Helen and Gillis Smith.

Photo Credits

Alexandre Bailhache: 47, floral design by Henri Moulé, interior design by Philippe Starck; 52 & 53, floral design by Henri Moulé, interior design by Philippe Starck

Anita Calero: 39, floral design by Zezé Flowers; 142–143, floral, design by Zezé Flowers

Bill Bolin: 68 & 69, floral design by Jamie Huizenga; 91, floral design by Jamie Huizenga

Brian McWeeny: 64 & 65, floral design by Lucy Diaz, interior design by Jan Showers; 86 floral design by Todd Fiscus and Raegan McKinney; 235 floral design by Lucy Diaz, interior design by Jan Showers

Briggs Edward Solomon: 202, floral design by Leslie Newsom Rascoe, interior design by Kathleen Clements; 216–217, interior design by Kathleen Clements and Briggs Edward Solomon

Casey Sills: 84–85, floral design by Johnathan Andrew Sage; 110, floral design by Johnathan Andrew Sage; 258–259, floral design by Johnathan Andrew Sage

Casey & Anne Sills: 264, interior design by J. Randall Powers

David Meredith: 99, floral design by Ariel Dearie; 105, floral design by Ariel Dearie; 160, floral design by Ariel Dearie; 257, floral design by Ariel Dearie; 260 floral design by Ariel Dearie

Don Freeman: 114–115, floral design by Lewis Miller; 248, floral design by Lewis Miller

Emily Followill: 56–57, floral design by Catherine Walther; 112, floral design by Catherine Walther

Erica George Dines: 10, interior design by Lisa Luby Ryan; 26, interior design by Betty Burgess; 152–153, landscape design by Jeremy Smearman; 176, landscape design by Jeremy Smearman; 215, floral design by Lush Life; 224 & 225, interior design by Beth Webb; 250–251, interior design by Jimmy Stanton

Erika LaPresto: 1, 2, 3, 4, 5, 6, 7, 15, 41, 94, 138–139, 146, 188, 240, 274, 283, 284, 285, 286, 287, 288

Francesco Lagnese: 58, floral design by Victoria Jones, interior design by Ruthie Sommers

Francis Amiad: 19, floral design by Pilar Crespi, interior design by Piero Castellini Baldissera

Francois Dischinger: 8–9, floral design by Raquel Corvino, interior design by Robert Joyce; 117, floral design by Raquel Corvino, interior design by Robert Joyce; 180–181, floral design by Raquel Corvino, interior design by Robert Joyce; 263, floral design by Raquel Corvino, interior design by Robert Joyce

Katie Stoops: 172, floral design by Laura Dowling

Kevin Allen: 109, floral design by Laura Dowling

Kelly Ishikawa: 125, 131, 141, 167, 178, 247, floral design by Jill Rizzo & Alathea Harampolis

iStockphoto: 15, 42–43, 94–95, 96–97, 146–147, 148–149, 188–189, 190–191, 240–241, 242–243, 274–275, 276–277

Laura Resen: 31, floral design by Miho Kosuda, interior design by Frank Faulkner; 36, floral design by Miho Kosuda, interior design by Frank Faulkner; 37, floral design by Tommy's Garden, interior design by Suellen Gregory; 60, floral design by Miho Kosuda, interior design by Frank Faulkner; 101, floral design by Carolyn Englefield, interior design by Greg Stewart; 196, floral design by Anne Foxley, interior design by Michelle Workman; 197, floral design by Miho Kosuda, interior design by Frank Faulkner; 208, floral design by Victoria Jones, interior design by Paul Wiseman

Lara Robby: 120, floral design by Michael and Darroch Putnam

Lisa Romerien: 211, interior design by Scott Shrader; 213, interior design by George Massar; 231, interior design by Vanessa Alexander

Luca Trovato: 151, interior design by Windsor Smith; 245, interior design by Clifford Fong

Mali Azima: 72 & 73, interior design by Beth Elsey; 132–133, interior design by Beth Elsey

Max Kim-Bee: 13, floral design by Nicolette Owen, interior design by Robert Bergero; 22–23, interior design by Furlow Gatewood; 55, floral design by Carolyn Englefield; 63, floral design by Carolyn Englefield, interior design by Kelli Ford; 71, floral design by Carolyn Englefield, interior design by Peter Dunham; 106–107, floral design by Olga Naiman, interior design by Frank Babb Randolph; 123, 124, 135, 155, floral design by Nicolette Owen, interior design by Robert Bergero; 156–157, floral design by Nicolette Owen; 164, floral design by Carolyn Englefield; 168, floral design by Carolyn Englefield; 177, interior design by Frank Babb Randolph; 198, floral design by Carolyn Englefield, interior design by David Easton; 204–205, floral design by Carolyn Englefield, interior design by Stephen Sills; 209, interior design by Richard Hallberg; 220–221, floral design by Carolyn Englefield, interior design by Thomas Britt; 226, floral design by Victoria Jones, interior design by Ann Sutherland; 232–233, floral design by Carolyn Englefield, interior design by John Saladino; 236–237, floral design by Olga Naiman, interior design by Vicente Wolf; 268, floral design by Nicolette Owen

Melanie Acevedo: 25, interior design by Adrienne Vittadini; 35, floral design by Victoria Jones, interior design by

Thomas Pheasant; 67, interior design by Nick Olsen; 102–103, floral design by Olga Naiman, interior design by Nick Olsen; 201, floral design by Susan Massar, interior design by Nancy Braithwaite; 212, floral design by Olga Naiman, interior design by Vicente Wolf

Michelle Vaughn: 74, floral design by Mary Jane Ryburn; 228, floral design by Mary Jane Ryburn

Miguel Flores-Vianna: 206, floral design by Carolyn Englefield, interior design by Luis Bustamante; 218, floral design by Pilar Crespi, interior design by Luis Bustamante; 223, interior design by Richard Hallberg; 229 interior design by Richard Hallberg

Oberto Gili: 183, floral design by Prudence Design & Events

Paul Costello: 195, interior design by Ann Holden

Peter Vitale: 45, floral design by Henri Moulé, interior design by Philippe Starck; 51, interior design by Jane Moore; 61, floral design by Jamie Huizenga, interior design by David Easton; 88–89, floral design by Jamie Huizenga, interior design by David Easton; 121, floral design by Jamie Huizenga; 136–137, floral design by Mary Jane Ryburn, interior design by Edward Holler and Samuel Sander; 184–185; 253, floral design by Johnathan Andrew Sage, interior design by Pamela Pierce

Rene & Barbara Stoeltie: 175, floral design by Jill Rizzo & Alathea Harampolis

Roger Davies: 83, interior design by Steve and Brooke Giannetti

Simon Upton: 20, interior design by Veere Grenney; 129, interior design by Michael S. Smith; 193, interior design by Michael S. Smith

Stephen Karlisch: 48–49, interior design by Jan Showers

Thibault Jeanson: 28, interior design by Alessandra Branca; 32 floral design by Marie Triboulot (Garance); 118 floral design by Marie Triboulot (Garance); 126, floral design by Carolyn Englefield, interior design by Suzanne Kasler; 128, interior design by Suzanne Kasler; 158, floral design by Marie Triboulot (Garance); 163, floral design by Marie Triboulot (Garance); 171, floral design by Marie Triboulot (Garance)

Victoria Pearson: 77 & 78, floral design by Danielle Hahn; 80, floral design by Danielle Hahn; 254–255, floral design by Eric Keosian; 267, floral design by Eric Keosian; 271, floral design by Eric Keosian

Every effort has been made to credit all of the floral designers and design professionals featured throughout this book.

Index

Note: Page references in *italics* indicate photographs and refer to location of photo captions.

HEARST BOOKS
New York

An Imprint of Sterling Publishing
1166 Avenue of the Americas
New York, NY 10036

ISBN 978-1-61837-179-9

Distributed in Canada by Sterling Publishing
c/o Canadian Manda Group, 664 Annette Street
Toronto, Ontario, Canada M6S 2C8
Distributed in the United Kingdom by GMC Distribution Services
Castle Place, 166 High Street, Lewes, East Sussex, England BN7 1XU
Distributed in Australia by Capricorn Link (Australia) Pty. Ltd.
P.O. Box 704, Windsor, NSW 2756, Australia

For information about custom editions, special sales, and premium and
corporate purchases, please contact Sterling Special Sales at 800-805-5489
or specialsales@sterlingpublishing.com.

Book design by Scott Russo

Manufactured in China

2 4 6 8 10 9 7 5 3 1

www.sterlingpublishing.com